Building the Practice You've Always Wanted

By Dan Cuprill

www.AdvisorArchitect.com

What people are saying about Dan Cuprill and Advisor Architect.

Kevin Wray, Wray Financial Services, Piconning MI:
"Implementing the systems outlined in this book has given me the freedom and profit I always hoped for when I became self-employed."

Nathan O'Bryant, O'Bryant & Associates, Jackson TN:
"Thanks to Dan & Advisor Architect, I am finally making decisions that translate into hitting a profit goal, and the results are incredible."

Greg Black, Tencap Financial Coach, Salt Lake City UT:
"The modern day financial advisor is an endangered species if he doesn't move away from the traditional way of doing business. This book is the blueprint for how to do just that."

J'Neane Theus, Theus Wealth Advisors, Columbia MD:
"How refreshing to learn insights from another financial advisor who understands business success goes beyond spending money on marketing. Working with Dan has given me the structure and discipline I needed to reach my goals. This book is a major breakthrough."

Chris Patterson, CPA, Patterson Financial, Ponte Vedra FL: "Learning the concepts in Advisor Architect is the single best thing I ever did for my business. I now have a systematic approach to growing both my planning and accounting businesses that will allow me to scale my growth."

Dan Betzel, Betzel Wealth Advisors, Columbus OH: "Dan is a masterful teacher. This book is not theory, but rather applicable information you can apply immediately into your practice. Do your friends a favor and give them all copies."

Brandon Stuerke, Creator, Automated Advisor: Of the hundreds of advisors with whom I've worked, Dan understands more than any other the way this business has changed and how advisors must adjust in order to survive. His work is essential reading.

Steve Lewit, President, L2 Advisor Strategies: Dan Cuprill is leading a movement to transition financial advisors from being just a salesperson to a becoming a true entrepreneur. Ignore him at your peril.

To learn more about Dan & his systems, visit AdvisorArchitect.com.

Nobody Cares if You're Profitable...But You.

It was an "a-ha moment."

The head of an insurance marketing organization stood in front of a large group of financial advisors. These men and women represented his sales force.

An insurance marketing organization, or IMO, is an insurance brokerage that contracts with independent financial advisors to provide them with insurance and investment products. In many ways, they are like a grocery store for the advisor as he meets the product needs of his clients.

Conferences like this one are common. They serve as a way to motivate the sales force toward hitting higher production goals.

"Don't worry about profit," he said. "Just keep selling and profit will take care of itself."

His words startled me. He had to know that this statement was blatantly false. If true, then Uber would be one of the most profitable companies on earth. Instead, it loses billions.

Of course, I realize and accept the profitability of the advisor is not the concern of the FMO. Nor should it be. And I don't mean to criticize just FMO's. The same can also be said for other vendors like turn key asset managers and seminar companies.

But until that point, I hadn't realized something which is now incredibly obvious to me:

The profit of an advisor runs counter to the best interest of his vendors.

A profitable advisor doesn't necessarily need to keep selling to achieve his goals, especially if he's built his practice using a recurring revenue model. But if advisors sell less, their vendors make less. So, it's in the interest of the vendor to always emphasize growth.

Vendors are necessary. The simple rules of comparative advantage make it wiser to fee out certain expertise rather than to develop it internally. Vendors allow the advisor "to be an advisor," creating ample time to meet with clients.

Nor are vendors evil. Personally, I work with some of the best. They are ethically managed companies that truly want their advisors to succeed. But success for the vendor (sales by their advisors) does not necessarily translate into success for the advisor (profit).

It's been estimated that only ten percent of those who seek a career as a financial advisor actually succeed. And those who succeed are NOT necessarily "successful." Common themes amongst advisors include personal bankruptcy, high debt, failed marriages, and poor health due to stress. I personally believe much of it has to do with the fact too many advisors focus on growth, not profit.

As caustic as it may sound, creating profit is the primary purpose of a business. Done wisely, profit is achieved legally and ethically. In fact, I believe seeking a profit is the single most ethical thing a business owner can do. It allows him to help more people, to raise his level of quality, to employ others, to give more to charity, to invest in new technologies, and dare I say...pay more in taxes (a bone tossed to those who feel it is somehow virtuous to do so). Few great things created by man were NOT the byproduct of someone seeking profit. The automobile, the cell phone, MRI technology, pharmaceuticals...these were not the brainchild of a centralized government committee, but rather an individual who wanted to make money.

If you see the pursuit of profit as something less than virtuous, then I strongly recommend you not be a business owner. You will fail.

Profit gives you freedom. Freedom allows you to impact lives. Profit allows you to hire people who can go on to raise their children and achieve their own dreams. Profit allows you to be more charitable, creative, and self - reliant.

As a seeker of profit, you are on your own. Other than your family (if you're lucky), few will come to your aid. In fact, some will actually resent you.

Do not be fooled into believing your vendors are your partners. Your profit is money you haven't spent in making them more profitable. As soon as you understand and accept this, you can start making wiser decisions to achieve real success.

Focus on profit within my own practice is the result of my business upbringing. I started my career working as an underwriter for a large insurance company. In addition to convincing independent agents why they should sell my products (yes, I was a vendor), I also analyzed the risks they gave us to insure. Despite doing well with that company, I hated almost every minute of it.

I knew early on that I was not meant for corporate America. Outspoken, I despised the bureaucratic ways in which decisions were made. Excessive meetings, emails, conference calls, and office politics. I did, however, receive valuable training that transferred well to being a small business owner. I also took advantage of my employer's tuition reimbursement program and pursued an MBA degree at Northwestern University to provide me with expertise my B.A. in journalism did not.

Then came Michael Gerber. If you've never read his bestselling book, The E-Myth, do so as soon as you finish this one. Along with my graduate school experience and time with Chubb, that book solidified my understanding of how **SYSTEMS**, not growth, create profit. It also emphasized that the goal of every business owner should be to become obsolete within his business. A true entrepreneur works ON his business, not IN his business.

It is with this knowledge I began my practice, Total Financial Planners. The first system I employed was a marketing system, Successful Money Management Seminars. SMMS is a complete turnkey operation designed to help you attract clients through educational workshops taught at local high schools and universities. We still use the system today.

Then came other systems, most of which I learned and adopted from others: an accounting system, a profit system, a selling system, a client retention system, a client mortality system (that's right...a system for dealing with the fact that clients someday die), a referral system, a staff system, and a succession system.

Success for me took its time in coming. I decided early on that my practice would be fee based, so rather than receive 5% or more upfront, I earn less than 1% a year on managed client assets (hence the need for a TAMP and their investment system). Two years in, my revenues were more than what I was making when I quit my job at Chubb, but my expenses took most of it. I was living mostly on the savings I accumulated over the past ten years.

I suffered through the usual small business side effects: insomnia, hair loss, high cholesterol, anxiety attacks, credit card debt, and the loss of almost all of my personal savings. But I never had much doubt I would succeed. Yes, I was personally confident (for the most part), but what drove that confidence was my belief in the systems I was using. Those systems were proven to work by others who were far more successful than me.

Today my practice, Matson & Cuprill, has over 200 clients and manages about $200,000,000 through third party asset managers. We generate revenue not only from money management, but also from financial planning fees and insurance sales. We do it all with a team of just three people: myself, my office manager, and an associate advisor I hired to eventually replace me. For many years it was just me and my office manager.

Like marketing strategist Dan Kennedy wrote, "Wealth is the result of systems."

When I started my practice, I wanted three things:

- To achieve consistently growing profit.
- To have a great deal of freedom in how I spent my time.
- To be able to someday sell my business for a huge amount.

Do you want these three things? If so, then write this down and put on your bathroom mirror:

Systems, not growth, create profit. Profit creates freedom. And people tend to want to buy profitable businesses.

My favorite system example is Fed Ex. The company's chairman, Fred Smith, created an airline dedicated to transporting packages, not people. Revolutionary at the time, he promoted the idea that you could send a package around the world and have it arrive in less than 24 hours. Today we take such an effort for granted, but back in the 1970's, it was mind boggling. Even with the invention of the fax and email, Fed Ex continues to thrive.

Think about all that is involved in sending an overnight package. First someone drops it into a mailbox. Then a predetermined truck driven by a predetermined driver picks up the package and drives it to a predetermined distribution center. It is then unloaded and assigned to a specific bin where it is then reloaded onto another truck and driven to a specific airport. It is loaded onto a plane and flown to Memphis, TN where is unloaded and placed on a predetermined conveyor which eventually leads to another plane. That plane flies to a specific city where it is then unloaded and placed onto a truck and driven to another distribution center. The package is then assigned a delivery truck where an assigned driver transports it to its final destination, gets out of the truck, and hands it to the addressee.

Every day millions of packages are sent around the world this way. And Fred Smith? He could very well be sitting on a South Pacific island sipping pina coladas. A system as well defined as his allows him to never work in his business, but rather on it.

In working with other advisors, I see so many who are lacking the systems necessary to achieve these outcomes. I eventually decided to share with others what I've been doing the past twenty years and created **Advisor Architect.** In the chapters that follow, I'll go into detail about the type of systems I believe every successful financial planning firm needs today. If at any point you wish to reach out to me, send an email to dan@advisorarchitect.com. I hope you do.

--Dan Cuprill

System One: Know Your Numbers

One of my favorite television programs is called **The Profit**. Every week entrepreneur Marcus Lemonis offers to buy a share of a struggling company in return for temporary, but total, control. If you watch enough of these shows, you will see a common reason why the featured businesses are struggling. The most glaring is a lack of knowledge about the metrics behind their business. Very few can explain why they aren't profitable. In one show, Lemonis showed how a restaurant's bestselling dish caused them to lose money with every order. They had no idea how much it cost to make it, and therefore had no idea how to price it.

At the most basic level, knowing your numbers is not overly complex. It simply requires you to input your expenses into QuickBooks as soon as you pay them. In the case of a credit card, you need to itemize each expense that appears on the bill.

Bookkeeping is not a task for your accountant. Rather, it should be done in-house so that the Chief Financial

Officer (YOU) can monitor results regularly. It's not overly time consuming. Neither is reconciling your bank accounts. Not sure how to do it? There are over a hundred videos on YouTube to teach you.

As a CEO, you establish the profit goals for your business. As CFO, you make sure they happen.

First Question: How much profit do you want to have in the next 12 months? Again, I said profit...not revenue. Write it down here:
$_____

What's your expected revenue for either the current or past year?

$_____

Now, let's look at your expenses:

How much exactly does it cost you to run your practice? Or put another way, what is the absolute minimum amount of money you would need every month to stay in business?

Advisor Architect members are forced to look at every expense incurred over the past twelve months. We place each expense into one of three categories:

1. Essential: To be an essential expense, it must meet the bare minimum requirements of what

makes a financial planning practice. For example, office rent, internet service, one support staff employee, telephone, utilities, and planning software. If you can think of another advisory practice succeeding without a certain expense, then it's not essential. I do feel one support person is essential because it allows you to focus on higher revenue producing tasks.

Essential Expenses: $_____

1. Image Builders: These expenses are a lot like luxuries. They're nice, but we could live without them. The subscription to the sales guru newsletter for $1,000 a year. The software that lets you analyze a mutual fund nineteen different ways. The membership to the Rotary Club that has never produced a single client. Brand advertising is an image builder.

   Image Builders: $_____

2. Waste: Waste is either things we buy and never use (trust me...you have them) or things we buy but don't work well (like lousy marketing).

   Waste: $_____

Got your numbers? If not, go get them. I'll wait.

The next step is to cut the Image Builder number in half. Remember, these are non-essentials. You like them, but you can live without them. Now, let's revise your profit numbers by subtracting out all of your waste and 50% of your non-essentials:

Revenue: $_____

Minus:
Essential Costs $_____
50% of Image Builders $_____
Waste $_____

Revised Profit: $_____

How close is your revised profit to your profit goal? Even if it's just $100 closer, that's money you did not have just a few minutes ago. I find, on average, this exercise frees up close to 10% in additional profit. I've even seen examples where the newly revised profit actually exceeds the profit goal.

Now, it's time to build a budget for the next quarter. I prefer quarterly budgets over annual budgets because they offer more immediate results as they prevent you from procrastinating with the difficult decisions one must make to reach them. It's easy to convince yourself that exceeding your expense budget in January can be offset by more austerity in the remaining 11 months. In government, that's known as "kicking the can down the road." Well, there are no can kickers in **Advisor Architect.**

So, let's now build your budget. You know your projected revenue and your allowable expenses. Study each expense category. You can always take money from one category and apply it to others provided the total expense remains the same. For example, if I'd really like to give my office manager a much needed raise, I can reduce my travel for the coming the year.

Sample Budget

INCOME

Commission Income	60,000.00
AUM Fees	1,204,000.00
Total Commission Income	**1,264,000.00**
Services	<u>36,000.00</u>
Total Income	**$1,300,000.00**

EXPENSES

Bank Service Charges	84.00
Commission Payable	12,000.00
Computer and Internet Expenses	30,000.00
Entertainment	6,000.00
Insurance Expense	19,992.00
Interest Expense	44,000.00
Marketing	120,000.00
Office Supplies	9,600.00
Payroll Expenses	4,800.00
401K	10,000.00
Payroll Salary & Wages	300,000.00
Deferred- Beverly Hodges	<u>18,000.00</u>
Total Payroll Salary & Wages	**$318,000.00**
Payroll Tax	36,000.00
Total Payroll Expenses	**$368,800.00**
Postage and Delivery	6,000.00
Printing and Reproduction	1,200.00
Professional Fees	18,000.00
Rent Expense	49,200.00
Telephone Expense	3,000.00
Travel Expense	<u>24,000.00</u>
Total Expenses	**$711,876.00**
NET INCOME	**$588,124.00**

Once the budget is set, it's now time to input it into your accounting software. What? You don't use a program like QuickBooks? You just put all of your expenses on your American Express Card and then turn it over to your accountant who does the bookkeeping for you?

If that is the case, then we've just cut another expense. As of today, you need to do all bookkeeping in-house. Keep your CPA to file your taxes and answer whatever questions you may have as they pop up. But the simple recording, analyzing, and reconciliation of expenses is now the duty of the CFO (you) and your staff.

I can hear the objections now: "I don't want my staff to know how much money I make." Seriously??? They already know. If you worry they'll conclude you are underpaying them, then it's time to remedy that problem. Never lose a great team member over money. If they deserve to be underpaid, then they deserve to be fired.

I pay my office manager 20% more than the going rate for my market. In addition, I give her every Friday afternoon off, which is worth another 10% to her (yes, it's paid time off). She may leave me someday for a change in careers or because I'm a jerk. But it won't be to take a lateral job that pays more. There isn't one.

Back to expenses. Okay...I get it. You're too private to let anyone see the company checkbook. Fine. You now have a reason to either get up 30 minutes earlier every day or to block off time on Saturday morning or Sunday evening to attend to the financial affairs of your business. If you're not willing to do so, then please close this book right now. You don't deserve to learn the rest of what's in it.

Still with me? Good.

By inputting expenses into accounting software, you can track the actual results and compare them to your goal for any time frame you wish. And guess what? That's exactly what you will do the first calendar day of every month. It's called the "Budget to Actual Report."

You now have the tools in place to be your own CFO. Again, you need only 30 minutes a day to fulfill this role. Possibly less. But this activity will do far more to help you attain your short-term profit goal than sleeping later or watching Sunday Night Football.

The next step in knowing your numbers has to do with marketing. It's imperative that you understand where revenue and profits come from. Remember the example I gave earlier where the top selling item for a restaurant was actually losing them money? This is okay if you know for certain you will make up the difference with other products, but this is rarely the case. Unless of course you are McDonald's. The Golden Arches knows very well it barely covers cost with its burgers. No worries. Any idea where it makes up the difference?

Soft drinks.

Yes, even with free refills, McDonalds has a profit margin of 80% on its Coca Cola products. They also make a ton on rent since most restaurants are independently owned franchises who rent the buildings from the McDonalds. Ray Kroc knew where the money really was, and it wasn't in burgers.

What about your practice? When you spend money on marketing, what's your average first year return on investment? If you don't know it like your date of birth, then you don't have a system to track it.

Advisor Architect members know. We make sure of that. Doing so has allowed them to increase revenue while still offering competitive rates. They know which products and services represent their soft drinks vs. their Quarter Pounders.

Knowing your numbers also means knowing which marketing efforts make more profit than others. Notice I wrote "profit," not revenue.

Every advisor should track in detail the results

from his/her marketing efforts:

- How much did it all cost (by line item)?
- How many people registered?
- How many came?
- How many booked appointments?
- How many were qualified candidates?
- How many paid planning fees?
- How many are AUM clients?
- Fees & commissions by product/service?
- Average cost per new client?
- Average profit per new client?

If your goal is profit, then time spent analyzing your performance will always be worthwhile. If you don't know, then you could be losing money on your most popular dish.

Benchmarks: Advisor Architect members have three primary benchmarks they seek to achieve:

1. Marketing expenses equal 10% of revenue: They must spend 10% of revenue every year on marketing. That's right...they must spend it. In every other expense category, I will reward them for coming in under budget. Not marketing.

2. Operating expenses are under 35%. And this included 10% of revenue gong to marketing. So,

they must come up with a way to operate the rest of the practice at 25%.

3. 75% of all revenue is recurring. In other words, revenue is received every year from the same clients. The advisor doesn't have to make a sale in order to accumulate the majority of his revenue.

These are the benchmarks that define a healthy practice, one that is likely to sustain up and down markets, does not require a continuous stream of new clients to meet expenses, and can be sold for a high multiple of profit, not a low multiple of revenue.

System Two: The Profit Motive

It's amazing how the simplest of ideas can create the biggest following.

Mike Michalowicz is an entrepreneur and angel investor from New Jersey. He owns several businesses. Some became very successful. Others failed, which led Mike to share what he's learned.

An author of four books, his Profit First is a classic. Buy a copy today. It's included in the orientation package we send all Advisor Architect members.

Mike's message is simple: Remove your owner's pay, taxes, and profit from your business the moment you get paid. Put that money in separate bank accounts, one for each category. Run your business on what's left. By doing so, you force yourself to make the difficult decisions that will ensure your profitability.

Most advisors I meet do what I call "Bank Account Management." If the money is in the account, then it's fair game to be spent. And it usually is. Profit is more of an accidental afterthought, rather than the primary purpose for the business's existence.

Business owners have the best of intentions. They want to be profitable. They don't want to accumulate debt. They want to have wealth outside of their business. So, they set up a projection of revenue and expenses and promise to do their best to live by it. But then reality hits. Like a New Year's resolution, it's back to old habits.

GAAP is CRAP

Generally Accepted Accounting Principles (GAAP) define profit this way:

Revenue – Expense = Profit.

This formula may work in accounting, but it runs contrary to human nature. By reversing the formula, we establish a priority we are much more likely to achieve:

Revenue – Profit = Expense

Or even better:

Revenue - Profit - Owner's Pay - Taxes = Operating Expense.

Now Operating Expense is the afterthought. Don't worry, the expense beast will be fed, but it won't take priority over the needs of the owner and the demands of the government.

Here is how **Advisor Architect** members put this system to work.

Once they have established their quarterly and yearly budgets, the owner now knows the amount of money he needs to run his business. This amount, divided by total revenue, equals the operating expense ratio (OER). Based on my experience and observation of other fee based firms, an OER of 35% defines a healthy practice, provided marketing comprises 10% of total revenue.

For example, Bill has a firm with $500,000 in revenue. To be healthy, he should have operating expenses of no more than $175,000 or 35%. Of that $175,000, $50,000 should be spent on growing the business. No more...and no less. The remaining $125,000 can go toward rent, staff salaries, and all the other requirements. By keeping this amount limited to $175,000 and not $500,000, Bill will be continuously challenged to find ways to cut costs and operate more efficiently. If Bill feels there is no way he can run the business on 35% (and he's cut all waste), then he sets a goal to get there by reducing OER each quarter.

What Bill is not going to do is simply kick the can down the road and delude himself into believing he'll get there through overnight growth. Instead, Bill will make difficult decisions over the next 12 months. He might terminate an employee or move to a cheaper office. He might cancel software he isn't using or discontinue expensive marketing campaigns that yield low results.

As much as **Advisor Architect** stresses expense management, it is not "ANTI-MARKETING." To the contrary. **Advisor Architect** is all about **Intentional Marketing** which we will examine in the next chapter. Marketing is an essential expense, but one that can easily get out of control. Kept in check, it allows you build growth and profit steadily. A budget of 10% of revenue ($50,000) gives Bill a healthy amount of money to grow steadily.

Bill now has 65% of his revenue earmarked for his profit, his owner's pay, and Uncle Sam's cut.

The next step is set target allocation percentages (TAPS) for profit, owner's pay, and taxes.

Revenue	$500,000	
Profit	$75,000	15%
Owner's Pay	$200,000	40%
Taxes	$25,000	5%
Operating Expense	$200,000	35%

To implement this **system** (there's that word again), Bill utilizes five different bank accounts.

Income Account: Every time Bill gets paid, deposits are placed into this account. Think of it as a serving plate onto which all money initially lands. Then on the 10th and 25th of each month, Bill moves all of the money from this account into four other accounts: owners pay, profit, tax, and operating expense.

Profit: Based on his revenue and personal needs, Bill feels he can achieve a 15% profit TAP. That's excellent. For some advisors, that amount is more of a long term goal. When beginning this process, I don't care if it's one percent. But it must be at least one percent. It cannot be zero.

Fifteen percent of the income account is paid to the profit account twice a month. The profit account is a savings account designed to help grow Bill's wealth *beyond* the value of his business. Yes, he may someday sell his practice for millions of dollars, but until he does, he should follow the advice he gives his clients: diversify. At the end of each quarter, Bill withdraws half of the profit account and invests it in his portfolio. He could also use it to pay down debt. The remainder stays in cash as a way to provide Bill with a buffer. In time, this will become unnecessary as he will build up additional cash reserves in business using a sixth account called **The Vault.** When that happens, he'll remove 100% of the profit account every quarter.

Owner's Pay: Bill sends 40% of all money in the income account to his personal bank account. This money is used for his living expenses. If he can live on less than he's taking, he'll assign that surplus to profit. While this program is defined as "profit first," in reality it's *owner's pay first*. There is a set amount of money Bill needs to support himself and his family. Once that's established, he then determines the other TAPS.

Tax Account: Situated in the lobby of my first apartment back in Chicago was once a restaurant called Mel Markon's. Nothing special, but it was extremely convenient whenever I had late night hunger. It had been there for years. I can still taste the French onion soup. And then one day...poof...it was gone. Not because business was poor. Far from it. It failed because it didn't pay its payroll tax. Federal officials swooped in one day and shut it down. Big brother wants his money now.

I've met a number of advisors over the years who have fallen behind in their taxes. In many cases, they had IRS liens placed on their earnings. These were not intentional tax dodgers. They simply lacked a system.

In the fourth account, **Taxes**, Bill sets aside 10% of all revenue specifically to pay his state and federal income taxes. Since it's 10% of the gross, it meets his obligation even though he's in a much higher marginal tax bracket. To avoid any temptation of tapping into this account, Bill establishes it in a completely different bank. As a self-employed business owner, Bill pays the majority of his taxes via four quarterly estimates. That money is now secured.

Operating Expense: Finally, we have the operating expense account. By design, it is indeed the last account. Only 35% of the revenue remains. It is the amount Bill determined he needs to run the business. Nothing more...nothing less. For the next 90 days, he is challenged to make due with what's in that account.

As the quarter progresses, Bill will become increasingly aware of his operating expense balance. It no longer has any fat. It's very lean and will most likely run out on the last day of the quarter. That's okay...that's what it's supposed to do. At that point, it will get replenished. In the meantime, Bill must make some difficult decisions. He must make the operating account last. This means looking for ways to lower expenses even further. Or putting off until next quarter some great ideas that have crossed his desk. It's not always a matter of "if" but "when."

Often, Bill will finish a quarter with a good-sized surplus. For example, let's assume he has $5,000 left in his operating account when the next quarterly fee check arrives. Does he add this amount to his next quarterly operating expense budget?

HELL NO!

Each quarter stands on its own. Bill must be rewarded for his diligence. The $5,000 goes into **The Vault.** The Vault serves as an emergency account, much like a "rainy day" fund. As that account builds, Bill is now better prepared to address the unexpected. He can even take advantage of an unforeseen opportunity without having to find the money somewhere else.

Bill has now progressed from running a sales office to owning a profit center. In less than a year, he will see his cash grow, and with it, his freedom.

For one day every month, **Advisor Architect** members become the Chief Financial Officer of their firm. They also become their company's bookkeeper. Some do so reluctantly. "That's my accountant's job," they say. Eventually, yes. You can let your accountant do your bookkeeping someday, but doing it yourself for at least the next year has several advantages:

1. It lowers your expenses, thus raising your profit.
2. It reminds you to cut waste.
3. It influences your profit-based decision making.

Once you're organized with a system, bookkeeping won't take much of your time.

System Three: Intentional Marketing

Financial advisors are a marketer's dream. As a group, we'll buy almost anything that has a chance to bring in more clients. Okay, I have no data to back this up, but being one myself I bet I'm right. In my career, I've dropped money on the following marketing efforts:

Radio Show   *Dinner Seminars*

Direct Mail   *Radio Ads*

TV Ads   *Referral Programs*

College Planning   *Wine (yes, wine)*

I'm sure there were more.

They all work...and they all fail. What's needed, more than anything else, is a strategy behind them.

As articulated by many, good marketing follows a three step process. You deliver the right MESSAGE to the right MARKET using the right MEDIA.

Alan Dib wrote a wonderful book called <u>The One Page Marketing Plan.</u> It's required reading for all Advisor

Architect members as well as the completion of the One Page Marketing Plan exercise:

What is Your Target Market? Get as specific as you can. In addition to age, net worth, and location, think of hobbies, political leanings, and fears. A lot of people worry that if they narrow their target market too much, they'll exclude potentially good clients. Not at all. The purpose of having a narrowly defined target market is to help spend your marketing dollars more efficiently. You position your message so that those you desire most are more likely to hear it. But there will be crossover. Every year people who don't watch golf, don't go to the theater, or don't make a lot of money still buy a Mercedes. Maybe they won the lottery or received an inheritance. They know they don't fit the Mercedes target market, but they'd like to.

A financial advisor who specializes in helping dentists maximize their wealth while lowering their taxes will also draw interest from the dermatologist and the guy who owns a chain of dry cleaners.

A well-defined target market is an easier one to find. Once we develop our message, we will know where to deliver it.

What Message Will You Deliver to Your Target Market?
Let's say I wanted to target middle aged dentists residing in Cincinnati. More specifically, I want to target only those who own their own practice. I conclude that the independent dentist faces some interesting challenges. As a likely high earner, he pays far more than his fair share of taxes regardless of what Bernie Sanders and Elizabeth Warren say.

But since he's a small business owner, he has at his disposal a number of tax planning options the W-2 employee does not. For example, he can choose from a number of different retirement plans, not just the usual 401k. He can employ his children, creating tax free income to fund their college or summer camp. He can rent his home to his business for 14 days a year tax free. He can establish a closely held insurance company, allowing him to deduct over $2,000,000 a year. The tax code has over 70,000 pages of opportunities, and yet so few small business owners take full advantage of them. Or I could emphasize to people with 401k and IRA plans that their retirement savings are a ticking tax time bomb waiting to explode. The former comptroller general of the US predicts that by 2020 entitlement spending will comprise 92% of all treasury revenues, increasing our debt by $3 trillion a year unless we dramatically raise taxes. If we raise taxes, then the amount we actually have in our 401k and IRA accounts will be decreased.

As marketers, we need to find the message that lets us stand apart from the crowd in a way that resonates with our target market. Intentional Marketing means becoming a big fish in a small, but deep, pond. Your goal is to be seen as THE EXPERT for your target market.

What Media Will You Use to Reach Your Target Market? Direct mail, Facebook ads, radio, TV, newspaper ads, billboards, website ads, magazine ads. Which form of media will most effectively reach your target market? What do they read?

What is Your Lead Capture System?

Unless someone calls you and requests an appointment, how else can you gather the contact information of someone who meets your target market and may want to hire you in the next year? Information marketing is a very useful strategy in lead capture. **Advisor Architect** members routinely offer free books, reports, and online courses as a way to capture leads. In fact, that very strategy may have been used to send you this book!

What is Your Lead Nurture System? Today's consumer is not likely to hire you immediately. Studies show it takes an average 8 contacts before they make a buying decision. How will you do that?

What is Your Sales Conversion Strategy? What systematic process will you use to convert them from prospect to an ideal client. I define an "ideal client" as one who will give you 100% of their money to manage and live with you through up and down markets.

How will You Deliver a World Class Experience? Here is where you can differentiate yourself from all other competitors. From the way your office looks to how you conduct client reviews, think of ways to separate yourself from all others.

How will You Increase Customer Value? Fee-based advisors must prove their worth every day, especially if returns are low. How will you earn your fee independent of returns?

How will You Orchestrate and Stimulate Referrals? Again, it must be systematized. I'll show you an example in System 6.

Advisor Architect members develop specific marketing

plans that address each of these issues following a detailed training session.

System Four: Kill the Caveman

For years, the idea of "selling" kept me from starting my own practice. I thought I wasn't any good at it. I possessed a huge amount of call reluctance and the fear of rejection. Deep down I knew it was in my head, but if I didn't believe I could sell, then I wouldn't.

Much of that changed when I finally discovered a marketing system that met my skill set. If I wasn't very good at selling, the right marketing system would compensate for a lot of my shortcomings. But even with a good marketing system, I wanted to find a way to improve my selling skills.

Wasn't there a better way than to push features and benefits and move someone from "unsure" to "committed?" Wasn't there a selling SYSTEM I could use?

I read just about every book on selling I could buy. Zig Ziglar, Brian Tracy, Tom Hopkins, and Joe Girard. All of these guys were great. But the more I studied their techniques, the more I started to notice what is now obvious: I'm not them...and I never will be. If they know the magical words, then God bless them. I don't. I needed a more systematic approach.

I found that system when I met Steve Lewit and later read his book, The Selling Chronicles. I recommend you read it cover to cover...three times.

Lewit's approach, which he calls "The New Science of Selling," is a complete 180 degrees from traditional selling. He focusses on the opening, not the close. He leads with the negative. He brings out all possible objections in the first meeting and lets the client do the closing. Best of all, he uses a system.

I call it "Kill the Caveman" because it forces me to no longer use the prehistoric selling methods of chasing, wearing down the prospect, and emphasizing features and benefits.

Advisor Architect members are taught that no matter what you do, a significant percentage of prospects are never going to hire you. They'll be happy to pick your brain and obtain as much free information as you're willing to give them, but they are never going to be ideal clients. As I described in the last chapter, *someone who will give you 100% of their money and live with you through good and bad markets.*

Today's client is fully aware he does not need you to buy

the products you offer. He can get everything you offer online, and probably for a lower price. The sooner you accept that reality, the easier it will be for you to move forward.

There must be a reason beyond buying products for the client to hire you. If that reason does not exist, then the prospect is simply there to get as much free information as you are willing to give him.

The prospect has an agenda. Hiring you may not be it. You can either get used, or you can make sure you uncover his intentions from the beginning.

Here are the main reasons the prospect won't hire you. I call them **Landmines:**

1. **He already has an advisor.** Yes, it seems odd he'd be meeting with you if he's happy with his current advisor. There are many people who cheat on their spouses but have no desire to leave them.

   Many people with an advisor will attend financial workshops. For some it's a hobby. Or perhaps it addresses an area their current advisor does not. Or maybe they just want a free dinner.

   The Ideal Client doesn't have a financial advisor. Or if he does, he's made it clear that he's willing to leave him.

2. **He's not emotional.** My favorite question to any prospect is, "On a scale of 1 to 10, where a 10 you sleep like Bill Gates and a 1 you don't sleep at all, how would you rank yourself as it relates to your personal financial situation." The bad prospect will answer with a 9 or 10. He'll tell you that he feels really good about his situation but he's interested in learning more. Or, he'll say that he'd like a second opinion.

   By contrast, the Ideal Client is emotionally driven to hire you. He's in pain, and he wants you to alleviate it. He may have $5 million, but he's still ranking himself a four or a five.

3. **He likes to be in control.** This is often the "do it yourself" investor who says he's contemplating whether or not it's time to hire someone so that he won't have to worry about his money any longer. Does he really mean that? Is he really likely to turn the keys over and let someone else drive?

4. **He's an Irrational Thinker:** He believes markets can be successfully timed or stocks selectively picked. Or he's unhappy with his returns, even though all equity markets may be down. He's

more concerned with what he has than what he'll do with it.

5. **Personality Conflict:** He's a jerk, and if he does hire you, you'll regret it every time he calls you.

6. **Takes Control of the First Meeting:** He has an agenda and wants to ask all the questions.

7. **Won't Move his Money:** The market is either too high or too low. Or he's worried about capital gains taxes. Or the stock that makes up 80% of his net worth is a family heirloom he just can't force himself to sell.

8. **He's Confused:** He doesn't know what he wants to do and has a difficult time explaining himself or understanding the process.

If you've been in the business long enough, you can easily recall prospects (and even clients) who had these traits. Rarely do they end up as ideal clients.

Advisor Architect members learn to not only identify these landmines (usually in the first 30 minutes of the first meeting), but also how to defuse them before offering any services.

The **Kill the Caveman System** provides the prospect with absolutely no information in the first meeting until it's very clear that the client has no landmines and therefore will become an ideal client.

If there are no landmines, then it's a natural conclusion the client will hire you. There is no need to close. He'll close you. At this point, an agreement is made to continue on to step two. For that, the client agrees to pay a fee.

Step Two of the selling system involves a design meeting between the advisor and the client to create the financial strategy together. By doing so, the client understands the problem of his current strategy and the opportunities that the new one offers. The advisor's role is to stress the pros and cons involved in each stage of the strategy.

Because **Advisor Architect** is all about profit, members seek to maximize revenue per client by offering holistic and unbiased advice for a fee. In addition, we assist our clients with the implementation of our recommendations, which results in additional revenue from asset management fees and insurance commissions.

In Step Three, the advisor presents the written plan. In many ways this is (by design) an anti-climactic stage as the client already knows what the plan is going to say having sat in on the design meeting. Done properly, this stage leads into a smooth transition of the client implementing the plan with the assistance of the financial advisor.

System Five: Automate This

When I first started my planning practice, several of my mentors recommended I hire an office assistant even though I could barely afford one. They argued I should spend my time doing $200/hour work while my personal assistant did the $15/hour work.

Today, my office manager earns over $30 an hour. Her time is very valuable, so much so that I can't afford to have her spend it on $15/hour work. I could hire another person to do that work, or I could use my computer. I chose the latter.

Office automation has come incredibly far in the last ten years and will continue to evolve. It wasn't that long ago when advisors pondered if their clients would actually use e-mail.

The automated systems behind my practice center around the client relationship management (CRM) system called Infusionsoft. I like Infusionsoft, but I don't personally endorse it. I'm sure the ideas that follow can easily be implemented using competing products.

In any case, I do recommend you use a software consultant to do most of the heavy lifting in customizing your CRM to your practice. Think of it like driving a car. You need to know only a few things to move the car from point A to point B. The science involved should be left to the mechanic.

Every day my office utilizes eleven automated campaigns to communicate with our clients and prospects. Most of them operate with little or no involvement from my staff.

Appointment Confirmation: We have four different meeting locations. In addition to our main office, we have three satellite locations throughout southeast Ohio/Northern Kentucky. Upon scheduling a meeting, a staff member completes an online form to indicate the date, time, location, and type of meeting. It takes less than ten seconds. The system then sends a confirmation email along with a road map to the office and a description of what to expect at the meeting. A reminder is automatically sent the day before.

New Client Experience: A new client receives a series of emails throughout the year designed to welcome her to "the family," educate her on our services, check in to see if she's pleased with our service, and even schedule her annual review.

The Investor Academy: As part of the "Client for Life" system, clients receive pre-recorded courses every 60 days with workbook downloads.

Long-Term Nurture: Prospective clients receive continuous email contact, much of it with embedded videos and limited time offers.

Robo-Referrals: A campaign that shares items of value with clients that they can share with friends through the system, allowing us to collect referral data. See system six.

Max Response: Most of our seminar attendees register via an email campaign rather than direct mail. The system sends them a confirmation, directions, and reminders of the upcoming workshop.

Ultimate Marketing Machine: By texting the word "retire" to 555888, prospects order our Retirement Rescue Toolkit, a box full of information on the concept of how to get a tax-free retirement.

Free Report: From our website, prospects can order a number of free reports. This gives us a lead capture element, letting us know who actually visited our site.

Blog/Podcast: Infusionsoft delivers it to over 1,200 clients and prospects every week.

Automated Leads: Social media ads offer free information to our target market. Infusionsoft delivers that information and provides a long-term follow-up sequence.

Thanksgiving Pies: Even mundane tasks can be automated. Via email and a web form, clients indicate which flavor pie they wish to receive the day before Thanksgiving. The system tabulates the orders which are then forwarded to the bakery.

Automation is not limited to email. It also includes texts, faxes, and even printed letters that require little or no human involvement.

Years ago, I attended a meeting where the speaker encouraged every advisor to set a goal of $1 billion of assets under management. The average advisor in the audience had less than $10 million of AUM with an average client account of $300,000. Using that same average client size, a billion dollars would require the advisors each attract over 3,300 clients.

I'm all for setting stretch goals, but the average advisor in that room was working out of his house and had no support staff. Do you think they could even fathom the infrastructure requirements of having 3,300 clients? Could most of them even handle 100 clients without a major overhaul of their workflow procedures?

Wouldn't it be wise to first build the infrastructure framework that would allow you to expand your business? For a relatively low cost, this can be done via automation.

Advisor Architect members receive the blueprints for building out such a system, along with the necessary content. In addition, my staff and I work closely with their technology consultants to ensure smooth implementation.

System Six: Robo Referrals

Many advisors I meet are like me: they don't like to ask for referrals.

I'm sure you've taken more than your share of classes on how to be better at it.

Even if you are good, very often all you get are names. There's no indication that these people want your help. They simply know one of your clients.

A referral is the most profitable way to obtain a client. Hence, a good referral strategy is vital.

Advisor Architect members use a strategy that solicits names regularly by first offering items of value that clients will want to share with their friends.

Value  Client Share

Value Items:

1. Free Reports: For them to be of value to your clients, they must be as educational as they are sales-oriented. They should also include a limited time offer.

2. Online Courses: Produced to not only educate, but also to highlight your firm's services.

3. E-Books: It can be yours or someone else's. **Advisor Architect** members co-author a book with me.

4. Podcasts: One of the most effective (and cheapest) ways to convey your message.

5. Articles: Again, either yours or someone else's.

Ideally you want to create at least six items of value that you can send to clients to read and share.

How your clients share the item is important. **Advisor Architect** members utilize a campaign within Infusionsoft that sends the material to referred parties. Along the way, it gathers contact information and provides a letter of introduction that notifies the parties as to how we obtained their name.

Going forward, we can now invite both our client and their friends to future events, mail out newsletters, send our podcast, etc. Like many of our systems, the goal is lead capture.

Content development is challenging for many advisors. Good content not only tells a story, but also has a call to action that motivates the reader. **Advisor Architect** members receive a number of reports they can use, as well as coaching on how to develop video and audio content.

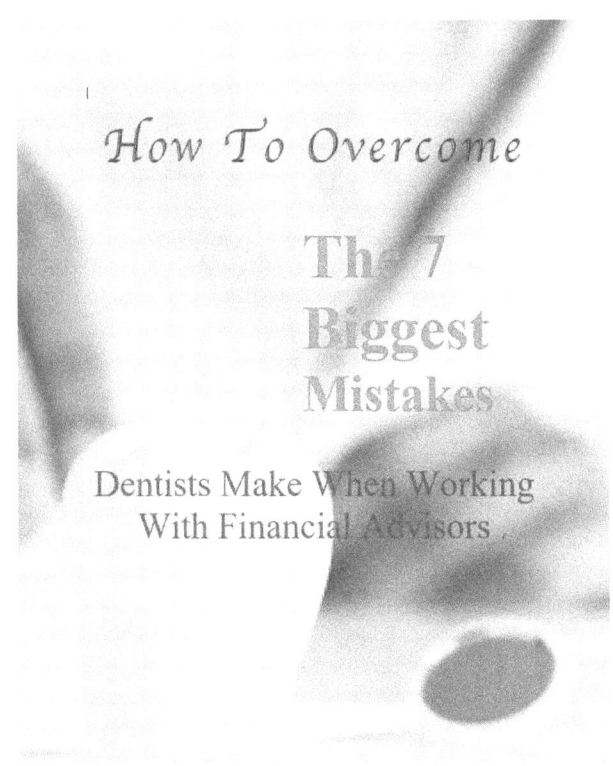

THE
SEVEN BIGGEST MISTAKES

WOMEN
MAKE
WHEN WORKING
WITH A FINANCIAL
ADVISOR

By Nikki Earley |

Matson & Cuprill

100 E-Business Way Ste. 160
Cincinnati, OH 45241
p 513.563.7526 · f 513.563.7597
www.matsonandcuprill.com
dancuprill@matsonandcuprill.com

Planning & Coaching for the Over Taxed

Dear Dan,

I recently published a book called <u>10 Most Expensive Tax Mistakes that Cost Investors Thousands</u>. The book offers in layman's terms an overview of our tax system and the way taxes can be lowered by using some very simple proactive planning.

If you haven't already received a copy from my office, you will soon. But until then, I have a favor to ask.

**10 Most
Expensive Tax
Mistakes**
That Cost Investors
Thousands

Daniel L. Cuprill CFL, CM, C, CFP

Matson & Cuprill
150 East Business Court, Suite B
Cincinnati, OH 45241
513.563.7526
www.matsonandcuprill.com

SHARE THIS BOOK   **ACCESS BOOK NOW**

I would love for you to share it with friends and family who you believe can benefit from its message. To do so, simply click here or on the link above to enter their name and email address and we'll email them the PDF right away. I'm confident they will appreciate it. I would also like to note that every time you refer a friend to this book your name is entered in a drawing for a $200.00 gift certificate to My Blue Ribbon Gift where you can choose a gift for yourself- just my way of saying thanks for educating yourself and spreading the information to others that you care about.

As always, please let me know if you have questions about the material!

Thank you!

System Seven: Client for Life

For the fee-based advisor, there is little or no profit without long-term client retention. That's obvious. You receive a small fee each month or quarter as opposed to a larger, upfront, commission. Profit takes time.

Too often the client relationship is based solely on returns. You are asked to prove your value based on how markets perform. Of course, you have no control over markets. You cannot skillfully pick stocks or time markets without information that no one else has. And very often advisors use returns as a way to attract new clients. It's a loser's game.

For the most part, a good selling system like *Kill the Caveman* can minimize these types of relationships. But even if clients hire you for all the right reasons, you will need to continue to add value once their pain subsides.

Advisor Architect members build a client retention utilizing a number of different campaigns and services.

- Pre-recorded Courses: Topics vary from "Choosing Your Investment Philosophy" to "Social Security Planning."

- Print Newsletters: The average person receives 144 emails a day, but only 6 pieces of mail from the USPS. Tangible information still works.

- Social Events: Murder Mystery Dinners, Plays, Winery Tours. Keep them fun and encourage clients to bring friends.

- Client Webinars: Half of my clients reside are not local, so webinars allow me to effectively communicate regularly and cost effectively.

- Charitable Functions: Canned food drives coupled with entertainment (comedians work best).

- Gifts: Where allowable by law as a way to say "Thank You."

- Podcast: One of the easiest and most effective ways to communicate with your clients. To listen to mine, visit MatsonAndCuprill.com.

- Plan Updates: A comprehensive plan grows old

very quickly. It is never intended to be a prediction of the future, but rather a projection as to the direction the client is headed. Much like a long airplane flight, it is always off course and will require constant adjustment. By continuously updating the plan, the advisor provides an ongoing level of service that speaks to the client's primary concern: will he have the income he needs throughout retirement? Be sure to deliver and review this plan in person.

System Eight: Generations

Do you know your average client's age? Don't guess. You either know it or you don't. When you finish this book, find out.

Let's assume it's 66. Now, what's your age? I'm 53. This means that, on average, I will lose my clients to death by the time I reach age 67. That's a problem.

Now, I'm well aware they won't all be dead by age 80. But possibly half will. The other half, on average, won't be too far away.

Obtaining younger clients is a good solution, especially those with money. How do we find them? How about the children of your existing clients?

The **Generations Program** within **Advisor Architect** utilizes a system that converts the future heirs of your clients into clients themselves by addressing a topic that parents dread having with their children. It's a talk almost as unpleasant as the one about the facts of life: Death.

Every year **Advisor Architect** members request a select group of clients to organize a family meeting. The matriarchs and patriarchs invite their children to attend a full day workshop with their advisor to learn their planning strategy and how it will impact them later in life when they inherit the assets. Often this is the first time they've seen how much their parents are worth.

They learn how the planning strategy meets their needs, the steps taken to protect them against the cost of custodial care, the tax plans that are in place, and the role each family member will play when it is time to pass the assets to the next generation.

Following that, **Advisor Architect** members conduct one-on-one consultations with each adult child. In advance of the meeting, the children submit fact finders, enabling the advisor to complete an analysis similar to what's been done for their parents.

This service, for which there is a charge, establishes an incredible connection between the children and the advisor. They now know who to call when their parents reach their decline in life. Even more so, they have started the basis of what is usually a long-term relationship. The advisor is now positioned to make the adult child a client as well, usually with very little effort.

To encourage clients to participate, we send them in advance a summary of the program:

What is GENERATIONS?

The implementation of an estate plan can be a very arduous and painful process. Grieving family members must deal with numerous time-consuming issues: wealth transfer, income and federal estate taxes, insurance claims, outstanding debts, new responsibilities, the re-titling of property and guardianship. Too often, heirs are unaware of these issues and how they will impact them personally. **Generations** *is a comprehensive program designed to educate the heirs of our clients on the estate planning program that their parents/grandparents created. It articulates clearly how this plan will personally affect each heir, allowing the opportunity to make adjustments if necessary.*

Who should attend the program?

All adult heirs.

How long does the program last?

Generations is a full day (8 hour) program.

How does one prepare for generations?

Benefactors will meet with Matson & Cuprill to review the program in detail months before their scheduled session with their family. During this meeting, we will update your various financial statements, as well as review any recent estate planning changes. With your assistance, we will request that your heirs complete a confidential fact finder to assist with the wealth coaching process. Materials will be mailed to them well in advance of the session date.

Why do the beneficiaries need to gather their financial data?

Those assets, when transferred, can have a dramatic impact on the heirs. Not only in terms of what can be done with them, but how they will be impacted by the taxation. Too often, unprepared heirs incur taxes that could have been avoided with proper advanced planning. **Generations** will give each heir a customized analysis that will provided specific recommendations on how to address the imminent inheritance and responsibilities.

What is the program agenda?

Generations is broken down into four parts:

1. Overview: You and your heirs will receive a complete overview of your estate plan and learn how it will affect them personally. Heirs will learn how much they stand to inherit and what restrictions, if any, will be placed on the use of

that wealth. We will also review the tax implications facing them and the estate, as well as the responsibilities of each heir.

2. *Education: Attendees will participate in two educational workshops: <u>Separating Myths from Truth: The Story of Investing and Choosing Your Investment Philosophy</u>.*

3. *Customized Planning: Following lunch, each beneficiary receives an individualized analysis that measures the financial impact that the benefactor's plan will have. These meetings are conducted individually.*

4. *Revisions: After learning of the plan and the impact it will have upon them personally, beneficiaries are given the opportunity to voice concerns and desires for modifications.*

What if all beneficiaries cannot be present?

The program can be conducted if a majority of beneficiaries are present. Otherwise it is best to wait for a time when all beneficiaries are present.

What is the cost for the program?

The cost is $1,000 per family. In addition to materials, a catered lunch will be provided to all attendees. Should your family wish to conduct the workshop outside of Cincinnati, we will attempt to make such arrangements at no extra charge.

Remember...Death is undefeated. Don't allow the life of your business to be based on the mortality of your clients.

System Nine: Passing the Torch

You've implemented your systems and your profitability is growing nicely. Many years have passed. You now work on your business, rather than "in your business." You are now older than your average client, so they are more likely to outlive you. Assuming you won't live forever, what will you do with your business when you can no longer run it?

It's been estimated that 90% of all planning firms do not have a formal exit strategy. As I write this, it is expected that a recent Department of Labor ruling will require advisors to have a formal succession plan in order to meet their fiduciary standard.

Advisor Architect members implement written succession plans that typically follow one of three approaches:

1. Sell to another advisor for a multiple of annual fee revenue. Industry standard is between two and three times recurring fees. A firm with $500,000 of AUM fees can potentially demand as much as $1.5 million. Of course, there will be factors to consider. Who are the clients? How old

are they? Will they remain with the firm after the transition? Will the new owner be comfortable with the investment strategy currently employed?

2. Sale price based on a multiple of profit. Industry standards are as high as six times. Now you understand why I like profit over revenue. A $500,000 business with a profit margin of 60% can demand as much as $1.8 million.

3. Incremental equity sale to a partner. No matter to whom you sell your business, financing will probably be required. And, they will use your revenue to complete the financing. You should demand a fair interest rate. The longer it takes to complete the payments, the higher the rate. For example, I bought out my old partner for two times revenue payable over ten years at prime plus 2%. He now receives a check every quarter until 2023.

Personally, I don't have a desire to just walk away. In fact, I see no reason to sell the business even if I don't want to work in it any longer. Instead I have created an incentive system for my future replacement that gives her equity now and the ability to buy more whenever she wishes. In the meantime, I receive income for life or until I decide to sell her all the equity.

If she lacks the capital to buy shares, then I will finance it to her over time, increasing my cash flow by the interest charged.

As a minority owner, she is now entitled to a share of profits equal to her equity stake. If she wishes to own a greater stake, she can simply buy more equity. Over time, the value of shares should increase, affording me a higher and higher purchase price over time. This approach is better than the simple percentage of revenue which locks in the value at the time of the sale. Not only do I stand to receive a higher price by selling shares at increasing value over time, I also give her a reason to focus on profitability, as doing so will raise her share of company profits at year end.

For details on the succession process, I recommend you visit FPTransitions.com.

The important thing is that you have a plan. Your practice is a valuable asset, and even if you have enough life insurance to choke a horse, your clients deserve professional assistance if they outlive you. Failure to have a succession plan is a violation of your fiduciary oath.

Bonus Chapter: Marketing with "Shock & Awe."

The first time I ever conducted a seminar, I mailed close to 20,000 invitations and got 32 family units to attend. That's a response rate of about .15%.

The seminar company assured me these were good results. I spent $15,000, which means each attendee cost me about $500 per unit.

Thirty-two said yes. Nineteen thousand nine hundred sixty-eight said, "no." That's good?

There had to be a better way. At the very least, I was

going to try to find it.

Imagine if I knew who those thirty-two people were before I did my mailing. Rather than mailing out 20,000 pieces of junk mail to find them, I could have gotten away with sending out just 32.

But how would I do that?

When you conduct a direct mail campaign, you hire a list vendor to find you names and address of people who meet your target market: income, investable assets, home owners. What you can't get is a list of people who worry taxes will absorb their retirement accounts. Or that their investment strategy is highly flawed. Or that they'll outlive their money. How do you get a list of people who have a keen interest in what you do? Even better, how do you get a list of people with anxiety about their money?

People don't hire you for the products you sell. Maybe there was a time they did. That's no longer the case. Everything you sell can be acquired online, and your target market knows this.

People hire you because deep down they have some level of fear they want you to alleviate. If that fear doesn't exist, then the likelihood they will give you all of their money to manage for the rest of their life is nil.

So, if the ideal prospect is someone who harbors anxiety about his money, then an effective marketing campaign will play to that fear.

Rather than market a seminar, market a solution to that fear and then follow it up with a seminar or webinar that discusses the issue further.

This is where I find social medial advertising to be quite effective.

Almost daily, prospective clients in a targeted region see one of my Facebook ads. Here's one that tested well:

The ad addresses a major concern of my target market: taxes. They've been paying far more than their fair share for their entire life. They're ticked off about it, and as they approach retirement, the IRS has a huge lien on their savings.

After clicking on this add, they are then brought to a

landing page that has a video explaining the issue further. In it, I offer them my Retirement Rescue Toolkit as a way to learn more about solving this tax problem during retirement.

The kit contains my book, a DVD, a CD, a free report, and even stress ball. There's also a post card promoting my upcoming workshop.

Once someone orders the kit, they start to receive a great deal of "stuff" going forward:

1. My weekly blog

2. My weekly podcast

3. My monthly print newsletter

4. Invitations to all of my workshops and podcasts

Someone who orders my kit has a 10% chance of coming to one of my workshops in the next 12 months. Slightly better odds than what I experience with direct mail.

Since they already expressed an interest in what I do, they're somewhat pre-conditioned to learning more.

The Shock & Awe kit is a very effective way to conduct 24/7 marketing at an extremely low cost. We typically spend less than $10 per lead.

It does, however, take time to work. I don't recommend advisors abandon other forms of marketing, but rather add this spoke to their marketing wheel.

I also suggest you get help with conducting your Facebook ads. More and more social media advertising is becoming a sophisticated science. Anyone can post ads. Not just anyone can get results.

Instead, focus your energies on creating a quality Shock & Awe kit. Writing a book is a major undertaking, but not nearly as overwhelming or expensive as it once was. Same is true for things like DVD's and CD's. In total, your Shock & Awe kit should cost no more than $10 to produce.

Be sure to also create an automated follow up system. It may take a year or longer before an interested prospect is ready to reach out to you. Lack of follow up is probably the biggest reason campaigns like this fail.

In addition to things like newsletters and blogs, utilize a multi stage email campaign that makes a limited time offer.

For more information on my Shock & Awe kit, visit www.RetirementRescueToolkit.com

A Special Offer

I hope I have successfully demonstrated to you how a practice based on systems can create the profit, freedom, and equity value so many financial advisors desire. Look at this book as an outline for building your own systems.

Of course, doing so will take a considerable amount of time, trial effort, and money. If you'd like to jumpstart the process, I encourage you to visit AdvisorArchitect.com.

Many advisors have been able to jump-start the process of systems implementation by taking advantage of the tools I use every day in my own practice.

As a way to thank you for reading this book, I'd like to offer you a free review of your existing systems. Simply email at the address below to take advantage of the offer.

-Dan Cuprill

dan@AdvisorArchitect.com

Dan Cuprill is the creator of the ProfitableAdvisor.com blog and podcast.

His firm, Matson & Cuprill, works with over 200 families in 20 states. He has been featured in *USA Today*, *Financial Advisor, The Wall Street Journal*, and *The Cincinnati Enquirer* among other media outlets.

A Certified Financial Planner, he also holds the Chartered Life Underwriter and Chartered Financial Advisor designations through the American College.

Dan is the creator of **Advisor Architect**, a multi-system business program designed to help financial advisors establish profit based practices.

To learn more, visit AdvisorArchitect.com or email Dan@AdvisorArchitect.com.